RESPONSIBILITY

by N. Pemberton and J. Riehecky
illustrated by L. Hohag and L. Jacobson

THE CHILD'S WORLD

Mankato, MN 56001

Responsibility is a good thing to have.
But how do you become responsible?
What is responsibility?

Responsibility is. . .
doing what you're supposed to do,
when you're supposed to do it.

Library of Congress Cataloging in Publication Data

Pemberton, Nancy, 1946-
   Responsibility / by N. Pemberton and J. Riehecky;
      illustrated by Linda Hohag. p. c.m.

   Summary: Suggests ways to show responsibility, such as remembering
to feed kitty, eating one's peas, and wearing boots in the rain.
   ISBN 0-89565-418-0
   1. Responsibility—Juvenile literature.   [1. Responsibility.]
I. Hohag, Linda, ill.   II. Title.
BJ1451.P46   1988
170'.2'0222—dc 19   87-37557

It's remembering to feed Kitty and
give her fresh water—every day.

Responsibility is hanging up your
coat when you come in . . .

and it is putting your books back
on the bookshelf.

Responsibility is eating your peas—
even if no one is looking and you
could hide them under the plate.

Putting your chewed gum and candy
wrappers in the trash can, not on
the ground, shows responsibility.

When it's raining outside, responsibility
is putting on your coat and boots—
before you splash in the puddles.

When you agree to play in a game,
responsibility is being there on time—

even if that means you miss the end
of your favorite TV show.

Responsibility is buckling your seat
belt . . .

not touching the party tray . . .

and being careful with a china doll.

Admitting you broke the doll—and not blaming your little sister—shows responsibility.

When the babysitter doesn't know
how many cookies you're allowed,
responsibility is taking only the two
Mom said you could have.

And it's going to bed without fussing,
when the babysitter says it's time.

Responsibility is picking up after
yourself . . .

sometimes twice.

Responsibility is making your bed . . .

and saying "thank you" when someone
gives you something special.

Looking out for a younger child—that's
responsibility. You can hold his hand
and remind him to look both ways
before crossing the street . . .

and you can give him a boost when
you see he can't reach the water
fountain by himself.

Putting your bike away, not leaving
it in the driveway, shows responsibility . . .

and so does helping someone in need.

Responsibility is thinking of others,
not just yourself.

When you are responsible,
others can count on you to do
what is right.